United States
Department of
Agriculture

Forest Service

Southern
Research Station

Resource Bulletin
SRS–172

Georgia Harvest and Utilization Study, 2009

James W. Bentley

The Author:

James W. Bentley, Resource Forester, U.S. Forest Service, Southern Research Station, Knoxville, TN 37919.

May 2011

Southern Research Station
200 W.T. Weaver Blvd.
Asheville, NC 28804

Foreword

This resource bulletin describes the principal findings of a harvest and utilization study conducted during the ninth inventory of Georgia's forest resources. Survey crews sampled and measured trees harvested in a variety of logging operations, and analysts calculated wood volume and percent of wood utilization. Harvest volume data and factors for growing-stock and nongrowing-stock logging residue are described and interpreted.

Annual surveys of America's forest resources are mandated by the Agricultural Research, Extension, and Education Reform Act of 1998 (1998 Farm Bill). Surveys and utilization studies are part of a continuing, nationwide undertaking by regional experiment stations of the Forest Service, U.S. Department of Agriculture. Inventories and utilization studies of the 13 Southern States (Alabama, Arkansas, Florida, Georgia, Kentucky, Louisiana, Mississippi, North Carolina, Oklahoma, South Carolina, Tennessee, Texas, and Virginia) and the Commonwealth of Puerto Rico are conducted by the Southern Research Station, Forest Inventory and Analysis (FIA) Research Work Unit. Unit headquarters is in Knoxville, TN, and FIA has operational offices in Asheville, NC, and Starkville, MS. The primary objective of these appraisals is to develop and maintain resource information needed to formulate sound forest policies and programs. More information about Forest Service resource inventories

is available in "The Enhanced Forest Inventory and Analysis Program—National Sampling Design and Estimation Procedures" (Bechtold and Patterson 2005).

Tabular data included in FIA resource bulletins present a comprehensive array of forest resource statistics, but additional information is available to those who require more specific information. Access to data for the Southern States can be found at: http://srsfia2.fs.fed.us/data/index.shtml.

Acknowledgments

The authors thank Druid Preston and Risher Willard for their review and comments; Anne Jenkins, Janet Griffin, Carolyn Steppleton, and Sharon Johnson for the map, tables, graphs, statistical checking, and styling; and the Southern Research Station (SRS) Technical Publications Team for editorial review, and publication of this report.

The SRS gratefully acknowledges the cooperation and assistance of the Georgia Forestry Commission in collecting harvest and utilization data. Appreciation is also extended to forest industry and loggers for allowing access to their land and logging operations.

Contents

[a] All tables in this report are available in Microsoft® Excel workbook files. Upon request, these files will be supplied on compact disc.

The use of trade or firm names in this publication is for reader information and does not imply endorsement by the U.S. Department of Agriculture of any product or service.

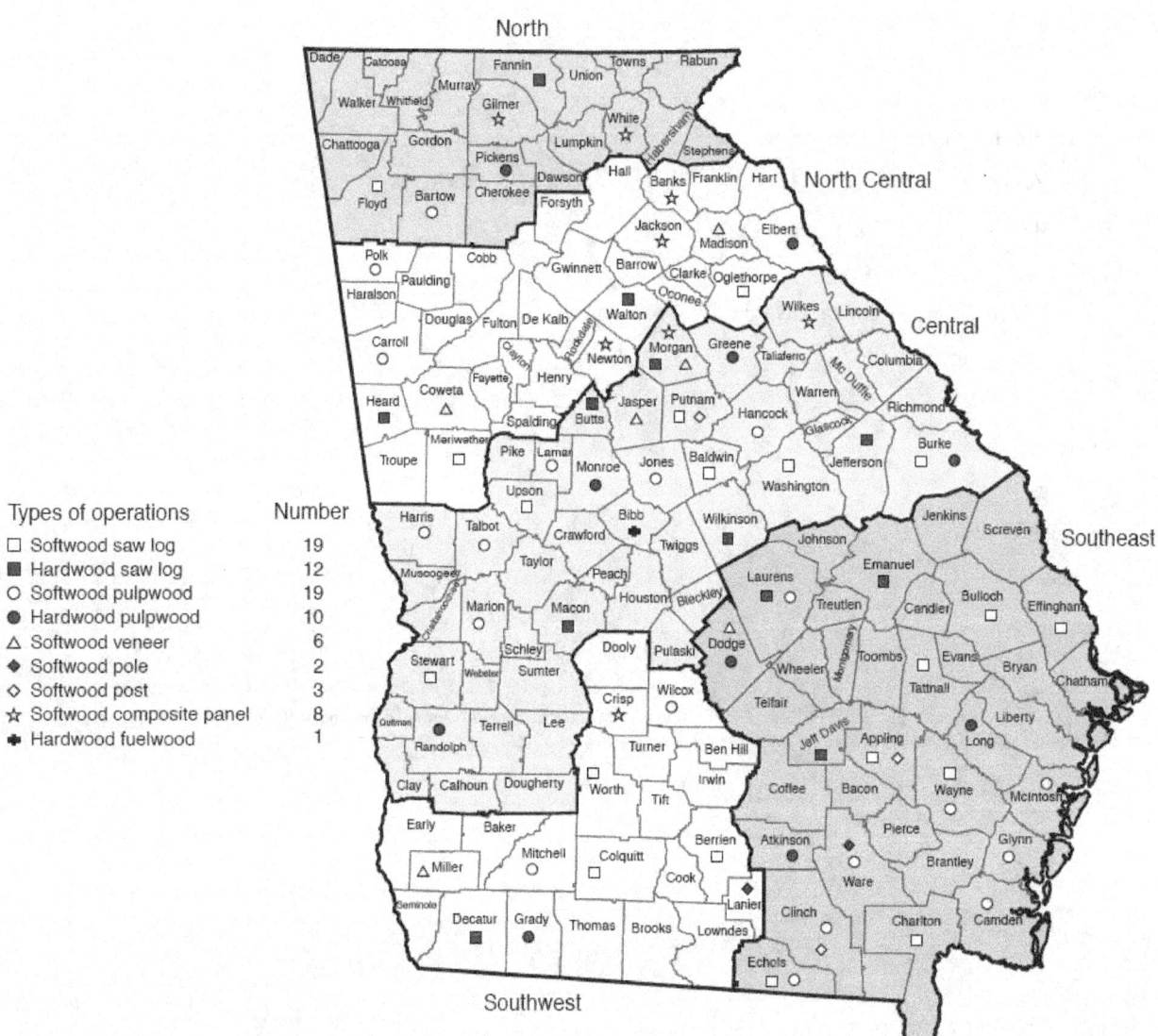

Figure 1—Harvest operations, Georgia, 2009.

Georgia Harvest and Utilization Study, 2009

James W. Bentley

Introduction

Forest planners and managers have a continuing need for information about the timber resource, and the public is expressing increasing interest in the effects of logging. Therefore, up-to-date data on the Nation's forests—and how the forests are changing—are essential to well informed decisionmaking. Information about the condition of and changes in the timber resource of Georgia comes from three primary sources: (1) inventory plots, which describe current conditions and quantify changes due to mortality, growth, removals, and land use; (2) mill surveys, which quantify timber volume harvested and delivered to primary wood products facilities, i.e., sawmills, pulpmills, veneer mills, composite panel mills, and pole mills; and (3) logging utilization studies, which characterize harvest operations and quantify the timber volume that is cut and utilized, and that portion that is left in the forest.

This bulletin presents the findings of a 2009 harvest and utilization study in Georgia. The study's main goal was to provide an estimate of softwood and hardwood volume used, and of volume left in the woods as logging residue. Survey crews randomly selected and measured felled trees on 80 active harvest operations throughout Georgia (fig. 1). This bulletin also provides some general characteristics of trees harvested for various products, examples of which are average diameter at breast height (d.b.h.) by product, average bole length by product, average heights of residual stumps, and average diameter outside bark (d.o.b.) at the end of utilization.

Some standard Forest Inventory and Analysis (FIA) terms are used in this study. Two of particular importance for understanding and interpreting study results are growing stock and nongrowing stock. A growing-stock tree is a live tree of commercial species that either contains or is capable of producing at least one 12-foot or two 8-foot logs in the saw-log portion of the bole. A nongrowing-stock tree is one that does not meet the requirements of growing stock due to poor form or rot. For growing-stock trees, the growing-stock portion of a tree (5 inches d.b.h. or larger) includes the volume of sound wood between a 1-foot stump and a 4-inch top, d.o.b. Volume in the 1-foot stump, volume in the main stem from 4 inches to the growing top of the tree, and the volume of any limbs 4 inches or larger with at least one 5-foot section are considered nongrowing-stock volume by FIA standards. Rough or rotten trees were also sampled and makeup another piece of nongrowing-stock (cull) volume. Figure 2 illustrates a poletimber tree, a sawtimber tree, and the growing-stock section of each.

Methods

Site Stratification and Selection

Producing a complete list of timber-harvesting operations and ownerships in a State such as Georgia is problematic. Because of the complexity of the timber industry, it is impossible to list the names and locations of all during the timeframe considered in this resource bulletin. Many uncontrollable factors affect how, when, and where harvesting operations take place, but the most common events that affect harvesting operations are weather and timber markets. A random sample provides a reasonably accurate estimate of utilization.

The sites selected for study were stratified by species group and product using the most recent data available for county-level output of timber products harvested in Georgia by species group (Schiller and others 2009). Using those proportions, 57 of the 80 selected sites were designated as softwood operations and the remaining 23 as hardwood operations. The same guidelines were used to designate harvest operations by product but allow for more flexibility because of the difficulty in locating harvesting operations for some products. Table 1 shows the final breakdown number of harvest operations, total trees, trees planted, and percentage of trees planted by product and species group.

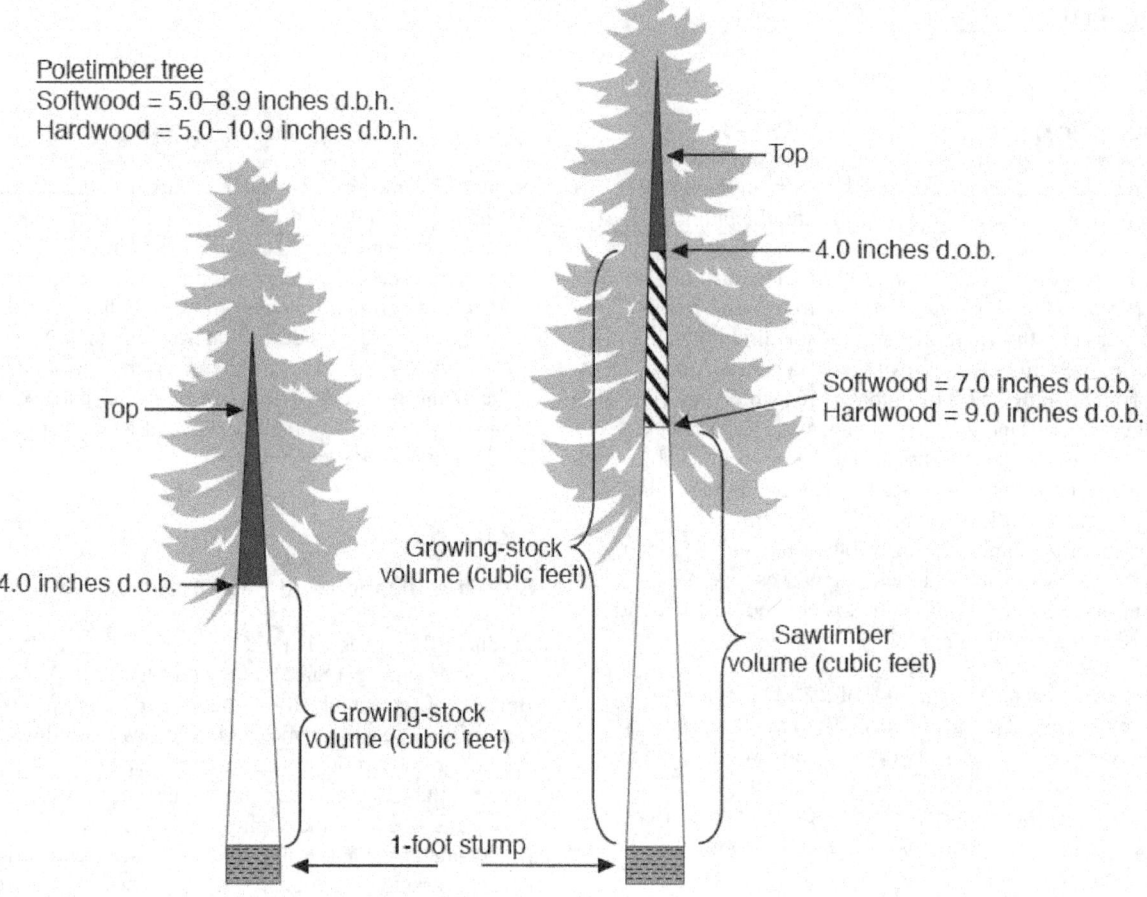

Figure 2 — Stem sections of poletimber and sawtimber trees.

After the harvest operations were stratified by major species group and product, the operations were placed in the appropriate region and county in the State. Using county-level product output data (Schiller and others 2009) and a map showing current mill locations, prospective utilization sites were selected based on a high probability of locating a harvesting operation for the particular product and species group assigned. Figure 1 shows where the final harvest operations considered in this bulletin were located.

Data Collection

During the ninth survey, field crews were trained to collect data on felled trees at harvest locations. Using the list of operations and a map of sites, they began collecting data by county for the particular species group and designated product(s). Data collection was from October 2008 to February 2009 on active harvest operations. To locate active harvest sites, field crews visited local mills and consulted county personnel.

Table 1—Number of operations, total trees, planted trees, and percent planted by product and species group, Georgia, 2009

Product and species group	Operations	Trees		
		Total	Planted	
		- - - - - - - - number - - - - - - - -		percent
Saw logs				
Softwood	19	448	198	44
Hardwood	12	207	38	18
Total	31	655	236	36
Veneer logs				
Softwood	6	125	26	21
Hardwood	0	0	0	—
Total	6	125	26	21
Composite panels				
Softwood	8	205	149	73
Hardwood	0	11	0	—
Total	8	216	149	69
Pulpwood				
Softwood	19	569	410	72
Hardwood	10	290	37	13
Total	29	859	447	52
Poles/pilings				
Softwood	2	31	17	55
Hardwood	0	0	0	—
Total	2	31	17	55
Fence posts				
Softwood	3	75	50	67
Hardwood	0	0	0	—
Total	3	75	50	67
Fuelwood				
Softwood	0	0	0	—
Hardwood	1	20	0	—
Total	1	20	0	—
All products				
Softwood	57	1,453	850	58
Hardwood	23	528	75	14
Total	80	1,981	925	47

— = no sample for the cell.

At each harvest operation site, field crews talked to the logger or person in charge of operations. These contacts provided vital information about product(s) utilized, specific diameters, and log lengths the receiving mill(s) would accept, along with minimum diameters at the cutoff points for specific products. Field crews also noted the type of logging equipment used. This information was used to determine the level of mechanization for each harvesting operation.

The goal of the field crew at each harvest operation site was to measure 25 to 30 trees for each product. This number ensured an adequate representation of overutilization and underutilization for a given type of harvest operation. Trees were randomly selected and had to be at least 5 inches d.b.h. and alive prior to harvest. Although often bucked, limbed, and topped, the main bole of each tree selected for measurement had to be intact to be measured for utilization. The State, unit, county, and location number were recorded for each site. Each tree was assigned a number and identified by species, d.b.h., tree class, product, bole length, and percentage of cull (if rot was detected). Each tree was measured from the top of the cut stump to the end of utilization. Measurements were made along the main stem in sections no longer than 16 feet until the end of utilization. The sawyer, according to particular specifications set by the receiving mill, usually determines the end of utilization. FIA merchantability standards for growing-stock volume are defined as the volume in the main stem of the tree from a 1-foot stump to a 4-inch top. However, most trees are not cut exactly at a 1-foot stump, nor are they cut off at exactly 4 inches. For example, trees cut off above a 1-foot stump and below 4 inches would be considered underutilized, and that volume not utilized would be considered growing-stock residue. On the other hand, by FIA standards, trees cut below a 1-foot stump and above a 4-inch top are considered 100 percent utilized, and those portions below and above are considered overutilization. A myriad of combinations actually occur on active harvest operations. The aggregated volume from measured trees has provided overutilization and underutilization factors that can be applied to statewide inventory results for an estimate of growing-stock and nongrowing-stock logging residues. Other required measurements, besides d.b.h. and end of utilization, are the top of the sawtimber portion (7.0 inches in softwoods and 9.0 inches in hardwoods). Those measurements allow calculation of the sawtimber and poletimber portion of the growing-stock section.

Highlights

Characteristics of Harvested Trees in Georgia

Results of this study identify several key characteristics of trees harvested. Such findings cannot be obtained from a typical field inventory or a forest industry study that supplies product output data only. Characteristics such as average d.b.h. by product, average bole length by product, average residual stump height, and average d.o.b. at the end of utilization is vital information for a full understanding of the complex nature of removals. Averages discussed in this section are based on the measurement of 1,981 trees, of which 1,453 (73 percent) were softwood and 528 (27 percent) hardwood.

According to Schiller and others (2009), softwood and hardwood saw-log volume together accounted for 34 percent of the total product output for the State. The study classified 448 trees as having softwood saw logs averaging 12.0 inches d.b.h. Forty-four percent, or 198 trees, were classified as planted softwood saw logs averaging 9.8 inches d.b.h.,

nearly 4 inches smaller than natural softwood saw logs averaging 13.7 inches d.b.h. It classified 207 hardwood trees as having saw logs averaging 15.6 inches d.b.h. Veneer and plywood constitute another component of the product mix for Georgia. Based on 125 trees measured for softwood veneer, the average d.b.h. was 14.2 inches. As expected, the d.b.h. of trees measured for pulpwood and composite panels was significantly smaller. Of the 569 softwood pulpwood trees measured, the average d.b.h. was 6.8 inches, while the 290 trees measured for hardwood pulpwood averaged 8.0 inches d.b.h. Seventy-two percent, or 410 trees, of the softwood pulpwood trees were planted, averaging 6.8 inches d.b.h., little difference in d.b.h. when compared to trees that come from natural stands. Two hundred five trees were measured for softwood composite panels averaging 7.9 inches d.b.h. Table 2 shows the average d.b.h. for each product by species group.

Table 2—Average diameter at breast height by species group, stand origin, and product, Georgia, 2009

Species group and stand origin	Product						
	Saw logs	Veneer logs	Composite panels	Pulp-wood	Poles/ pilings	Fence posts	Fuel-wood
	inches						
Softwood							
Natural	13.71	13.61	8.68	6.81	14.39	7.54	—
Planted	9.84	16.58	7.60	6.76	11.51	6.14	—
Total	12.00	14.23	7.89	6.77	12.81	6.60	—
Hardwood							
Natural	15.86	—	7.67	7.96	—	—	—
Planted	14.56	—	—	7.90	—	—	7.78
Total	15.62	—	7.67	7.95	—	—	7.78

— = no sample for the cell.

Bole length is the distance between a 1-foot stump and a 4-inch top. As expected, trees harvested for solid wood products tended to have longer average bole lengths than trees harvested for pulpwood or composite panel products. The average bole length for softwood trees measured for saw logs was 59 feet, while trees measured for hardwood saw logs had an average bole length of 61 feet. In comparison, trees measured for pulpwood had average bole lengths of 29 feet for softwoods and 34 feet for hardwoods. Softwood veneer trees had an average bole length of 69 feet. Planted sites constituted a subset of all trees measured. Trees measured in planted stands tended to have shorter bole lengths than those measured in the natural stands. Table 3 shows the average bole length by species group.

Residual stump height is a key component in determining utilization rates for harvested trees. By FIA standards, the stump is that portion of the tree measured at ground level from the uphill side of the tree to 1 foot up the bole. Loggers try to maximize volume harvested by cutting the tree as close to the ground as possible. Residual stump heights across the products ranged from 0.15 to 0.72 foot; however, most softwood trees harvested had an average residual stump height of about 0.40 foot or less, while harvested hardwood trees averaged slightly higher residual stumps. In softwoods and across all products, this accounted for about 49 percent of the stump volume being utilized. In hardwoods and across all products, about 27 percent of stump volume was used. Stump volume for both hardwood and softwood contributed to utilization of the nongrowing-stock portion of trees, i.e., overutilization. Residual stump heights for trees coming from natural stands appear slightly higher than residual stump heights in planted stands. Table 4 shows the average residual stump heights for each product by species group.

The final component we used to determine use rates was d.o.b. at the end of utilization. Tops and limbs constitute most of the nongrowing-stock volume; they accounted for 47 percent of the nongrowing-stock portion that was utilized. The average end of utilization for softwood saw logs was 4.1 inches, and for hardwood saw logs 6.0 inches. The average end of utilization for softwood and hardwood pulpwood was 2.2 and 3.3 inches, respectively. Trees coming from natural and planted stands showed almost no difference in the end of utilization. Table 5 shows the average end of utilization by the different products and species group.

Table 3—Average bole length by species group, stand origin, and product, Georgia, 2009

Species group and stand origin	Saw logs	Veneer logs	Composite panels	Pulp-wood	Poles/pilings	Fence posts	Fuel-wood
				feet			
Softwood							
Natural	64.93	67.46	46.48	30.14	70.93	41.56	—
Planted	51.25	76.85	35.19	29.18	70.88	29.00	—
Total	58.83	69.42	38.28	29.45	70.90	33.19	—
Hardwood							
Natural	62.22	—	27.91	34.09	—	—	34.75
Planted	57.39	—	—	33.14	—	—	—
Total	61.34	—	27.91	33.97	—	—	34.75

— = no sample for the cell.

Table 4—Average residual stump height by species group, stand origin, and product, Georgia, 2009

Species group and stand origin	Saw logs	Veneer logs	Composite panels	Pulp-wood	Poles/ pilings	Fence posts	Fuel-wood
				feet			
Softwood							
Natural	0.44	0.52	0.61	0.32	0.30	0.48	—
Planted	0.28	0.61	0.46	0.28	0.27	0.15	—
Total	0.37	0.54	0.50	0.29	0.28	0.26	—
Hardwood							
Natural	0.72	—	0.57	0.48	—	—	0.40
Planted	0.46	—	—	0.36	—	—	—
Total	0.67	—	0.57	0.47	—	—	0.40

— = no sample for the cell.

Table 5—Average end of utilization by species group, stand origin, and product, Georgia, 2009

Species group and stand origin	Saw logs	Veneer logs	Composite panels	Pulp-wood	Poles/ pilings	Fence posts	Fuel-wood
				inches			
Softwood							
Natural	5.13	4.37	3.46	2.32	4.66	2.23	—
Planted	2.90	5.52	2.35	2.12	5.47	2.75	—
Total	4.14	4.61	2.66	2.17	5.10	2.57	—
Hardwood							
Natural	5.80	—	2.98	3.22	—	—	1.88
Planted	6.98	—	—	4.04	—	—	—
Total	6.02	—	2.98	3.32	—	—	1.88

— = no sample for the cell.

Characteristics of Logging in Georgia

When field crews visited the 80 individual logging operations, they asked the logger some additional questions. The purpose for these questions was two-fold: to predict the level of mechanization and to better understand a typical logging operation.

The information gathered provided data on the equipment loggers used and how they used it. Across the 80 operations, the average age of logging equipment in use was 4.7 years old, ranging from 1 to 15 years. Typically, at each logging operation, one rubber-tired feller-buncher with a sawhead was used for cutting down the trees. Skidding was accomplished with an average of a little more than one rubber-tired grapple skidder. Most of the delimbing was done on the landing with a pull-through delimber or near the landing with a push-through, gate style delimber. The trees were typically loaded with a knuckleboom loader averaging one loader per operation.

Field crews also noted hauling practices and productivity. The self-reported productivity ranged from 2 to 20 loads per day, averaging 9.3 loads per day across the State. An adequate number of double-bunk or pole trailers were most commonly used for hauling. Accounting for some sites being right beside a public road to others being miles away, the average distance from a public road to the logging site was 0.6 miles.

Field crews further noted preferences and characteristics of the loggers themselves. Most of the loggers were willing to travel as far as a neighboring county to work, but 37 of the 80 were willing to travel an average of about 50 miles to work. Some Georgia loggers procure wood for themselves, but most prefer working as contractors for forest industry or private timber buyers. All of the loggers in Georgia were required to be certified, and most were members of a professional logger program.

Softwood Removals

Results from this study document 26,028 cubic feet of softwood volume, of which 22,950 cubic feet, or 88 percent, was used for product(s). Twelve percent, or 3,078 cubic feet, was left onsite as logging residue (fig. 3). Twenty-five percent of the residue volume came from the growing-stock portion of the tree, while 75 percent came from the nongrowing-stock portion (stumps, tops, and limbs) (fig. 4) (table A.1).

The total softwood growing-stock volume measured was 22,642 cubic feet, of which 97 percent was utilized and 3 percent was logging residue (fig. 5). By FIA merchantability standards, the logging residue portion of growing-stock trees is underutilized volume. Of the total utilized volume, 1,080 cubic feet, or 4.7 percent, was from the nongrowing-stock portion of trees. By the same merchantability standards, that volume is considered overutilization (tables A.2 and A.3).

Softwood volumes and percentages are broken down further by poletimber and sawtimber, and by the various products measured (tables A.2 through A.9). By product, trees harvested for pulpwood had average rates of utilization for the merchantable portion of the tree (98 percent) and the highest rate of overutilization (13.8 percent), meaning that more of the nongrowing-stock portion of the tree was used for products and less was left as logging residue.

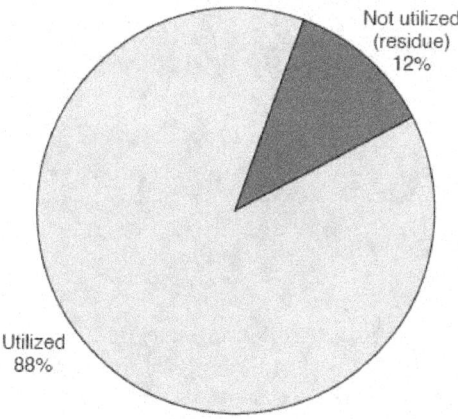

Total 26.0 thousand cubic feet

Figure 3—Disposition of total softwood harvest volume, Georgia, 2009.

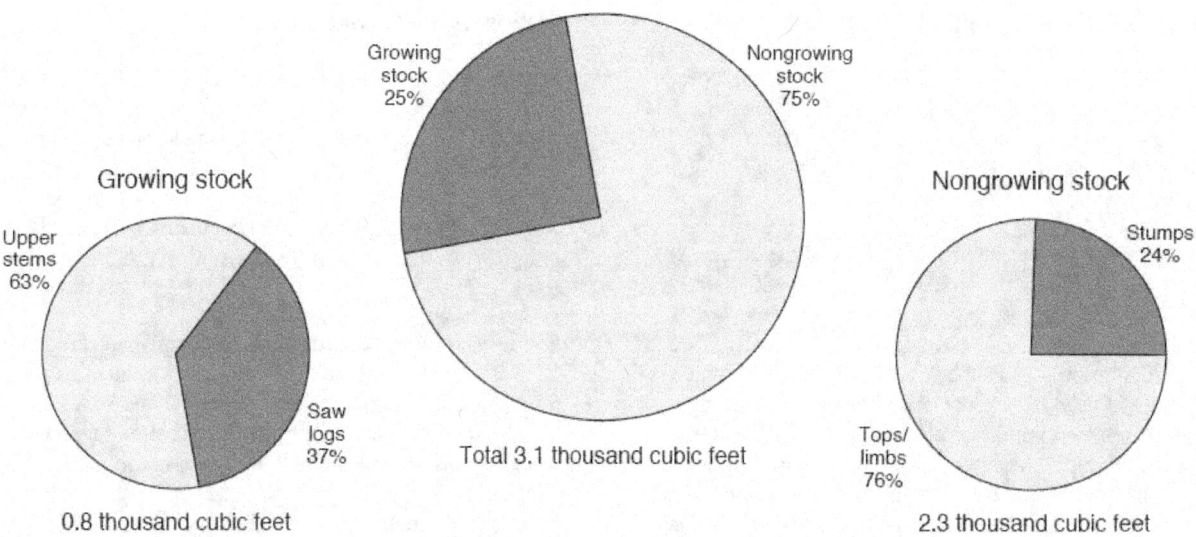

Figure 4—Softwood residue by volume type, Georgia, 2009.

Growing stock
Upper stems 63%
Saw logs 37%
0.8 thousand cubic feet

Growing stock 25%
Nongrowing stock 75%
Total 3.1 thousand cubic feet

Nongrowing stock
Stumps 24%
Tops/limbs 76%
2.3 thousand cubic feet

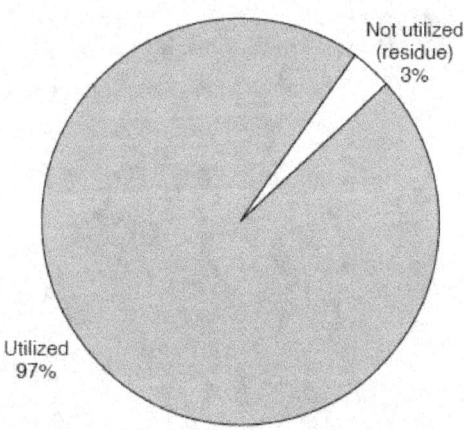

Not utilized (residue) 3%

Utilized 97%

Total 22.6 thousand cubic feet

Figure 5—Disposition of softwood growing-stock volume, Georgia, 2009.

Hardwood Removals

Results from this study document 14,258 cubic feet of hardwood volume, of which 11,084 cubic feet, or 78 percent, was utilized for product(s). Twenty-two percent, or 3,174 cubic feet, was left onsite as logging residue (fig. 6). Twenty-nine percent of residue volume came from the growing-stock portion of trees, and 71 percent came from the nongrowing-stock portion (stumps, tops, and limbs) (fig. 7) (table A.1).

The total hardwood growing-stock volume measured was 11,674 cubic feet, of which 92 percent was used and 8 percent was logging residue (fig. 8). By FIA merchantability standards, the logging residue portion is underutilized volume. Of the total utilized volume, 327 cubic feet, or 3.0 percent, was from the nongrowing-stock portion of trees. By the same merchantability standards, that volume is considered overutilization (tables A.10 and A.11).

Hardwood volumes and percentages also were measured for poletimber and sawtimber, and differentiated by the various products they provided (tables A.10 through A.17). At 94 percent, however, those trees measured for pulpwood were more fully utilized, and more of the nongrowing-stock portion was used for products. Trees measured for hardwood saw logs were the least utilized of all, although they have the most nongrowing-stock material.

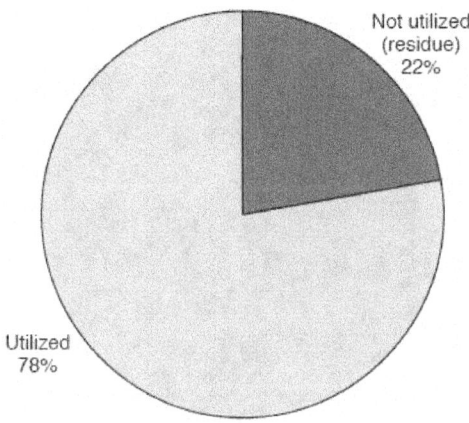

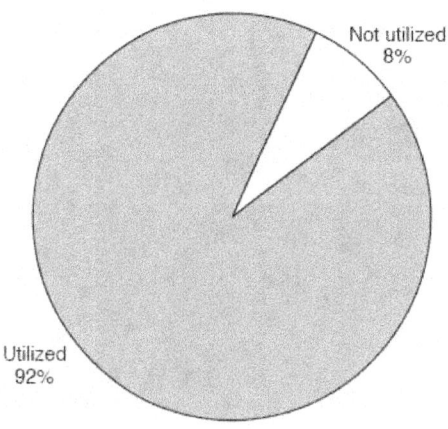

Total 14.3 thousand cubic feet

Figure 6—Disposition of total hardwood harvest volume, Georgia, 2009.

Total 11.7 thousand cubic feet

Figure 8—Disposition of hardwood growing-stock volume, Georgia, 2009.

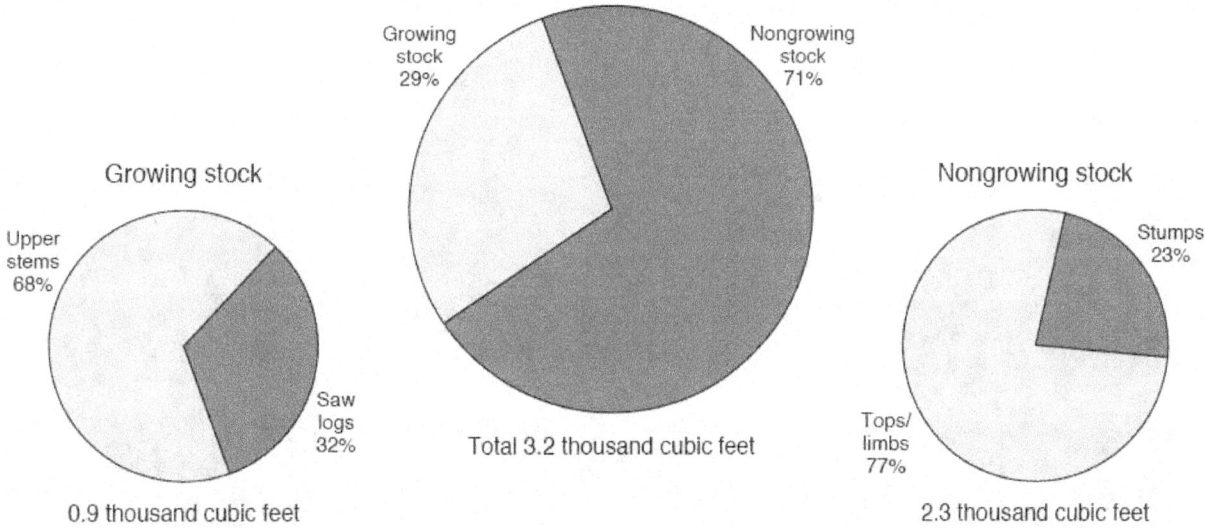

Figure 7—Hardwood residue by volume type, Georgia, 2009.

Literature Cited

Bechtold, W.A.; Patterson, P.L., eds. 2005.The enhanced forest inventory and analysis program—national sampling design and estimation procedures. Gen. Tech. Rep. SRS–80. Asheville, NC: U.S. Department of Agriculture Forest Service, Southern Research Station. 85 p.

Schiller, J.R.; McClure, N.; Willard, R.A. 2009. Georgia's timber industry—an assessment of timber product output and use, 2007. Resour. Bull. SRS–161. Asheville, NC: U.S. Department of Agriculture Forest Service, Southern Research Station. 35 p.

Glossary

Board foot. Unit of measure applied to roundwood. It relates to lumber that is 1-foot long, 1-foot wide, and 1-inch thick (or its equivalent).

Composite products. Roundwood products manufactured into chips, wafers, strands, flakes, shavings, or sawdust and then reconstituted into a variety of panel and engineered lumber products.

Drain. The volume of roundwood removed from any geographic area where timber is grown.

Growing-stock removals. The growing-stock volume removed from poletimber and sawtimber trees in the timberland inventory. (Note: Includes volume removed for roundwood products, logging residues, and other removals.)

Growing-stock trees. Living trees of commercial species classified as sawtimber, poletimber, saplings, and seedlings. Growing-stock trees must contain at least one 12-foot or two 8-foot logs in the saw-log portion, currently or potentially (if too small to qualify). The log(s) must meet dimension and merchantability standards and have, currently or potentially, one-third of the gross board-foot volume in sound wood.

Growing-stock volume. The cubic-foot volume of sound wood in growing-stock trees at least 5.0 inches d.b.h. from a 1-foot stump to a minimum 4.0-inch top d.o.b. of the central stem.

Hardwoods. Dicotyledonous trees, usually broadleaf and deciduous.

Soft hardwoods. Hardwood species with an average specific gravity ≤ 0.50, such as gums, yellow-poplar, cottonwoods, red maple, basswoods, and willows.

Hard hardwoods. Hardwood species with an average specific gravity > 0.50, such as oaks, hard maples, hickories, and beech.

Industrial roundwood products. Any primary use of the main stem of a tree, such as saw logs, pulpwood, and veneer logs, intended to be processed into primary wood products, such as lumber, wood pulp, and sheathing, at primary wood-using mills.

International ¼-inch rule. A log rule or formula for estimating the board-foot volume of logs, allowing ½-inch of taper for each 4-foot length. The rule appears in a number of forms that allow for kerf. In the form used by FIA, a ¼-inch of kerf is assumed. This rule is used as the USDA Forest Service standard log rule in the Eastern United States.

Log. A primary forest product harvested in long, primarily 8-, 12-, and 16-foot lengths.

Logging residues. The unused portion of trees cut or destroyed during logging operations.

Merchantable portion. That portion of live trees 5.0 inches d.b.h. and larger between a 1-foot stump and a minimum 4.0-inch top d.o.b. on the central stem. That portion of primary forks from the point of occurrence to a minimum 4.0-inch top d.o.b. is included.

Merchantable volume. Solid-wood volume in the merchantable portion of live trees.

Noncommercial species. Tree species of typically small size, poor form, or inferior quality that normally do not develop into trees suitable for industrial wood products.

Nonforest land. Land that has never supported forests and land formerly forested where timber production is precluded by development for other uses.

Nongrowing-stock sources. The net volume removed from the nongrowing-stock portions of poletimber and sawtimber trees (stumps, tops, limbs, cull sections of central stem) and from any portion of a rough, rotten, sapling, dead, or nonforest tree.

Other forest land. Forest land other than timberland and productive reserved forest land. It includes available and reserved forest land that is incapable of producing annually 20 cubic feet per acre of industrial wood under natural conditions because of adverse site conditions such as sterile soils, dry climate, poor drainage, high elevation, steepness, or rockiness.

Other products. A miscellaneous category of roundwood products, e.g., cooperage, excelsior, shingles, and mill residue byproducts (charcoal, bedding, mulch, etc.).

Other removals. The growing-stock volume of trees removed from the inventory by cultural operations such as timber stand improvement, land clearing, and other changes in land use, resulting in the removal of the trees from timberland.

Other sources. (See: Nongrowing-stock sources.)

Poletimber-size trees. Softwoods 5.0 to 8.9 inches d.b.h. and hardwoods 5.0 to 10.9 inches d.b.h.

Posts, poles, and pilings. Roundwood products milled (cut or peeled) into standard sizes (lengths and circumferences) to be put in the ground to provide vertical and lateral support in buildings, foundations, utility lines, and fences. May also include nonindustrial (unmilled) products.

Primary wood-using plants. Industries that convert roundwood products (saw logs, veneer logs, pulpwood, etc.) into primary wood products, such as lumber, veneer or sheathing, and wood pulp.

Pulpwood. A roundwood product that will be reduced to individual wood fibers by chemical or mechanical means. The fibers are used to make a broad generic group of pulp products that includes paper products, as well as chipboard, fiberboard, insulating board, and paperboard.

Rotten trees. Live trees of commercial species not containing at least one 12-foot saw log, or two noncontiguous saw logs, each 8 feet or longer, now or prospectively, primarily because of rot or missing sections, and with less than one-third of the gross board-foot tree volume in sound material.

Rough trees. Live trees of commercial species not containing at least one 12-foot saw log, or two noncontiguous saw logs, each 8 feet or longer, now or prospectively, primarily because of roughness, poor form, splits, and cracks, and with less than one-third of the gross board-foot tree volume in sound material; and live trees of noncommercial species.

Roundwood (roundwood logs). Logs, bolts, or other round sections cut from trees for industrial manufacture or consumer uses.

Roundwood chipped. Any timber cut primarily for industrial manufacture, delivered to nonpulpmills, chipped, and then sold to pulpmills for use as fiber. Includes tops, jump sections, whole trees, and pulpwood sticks.

Roundwood product drain. That portion of total drain used for a product.

Roundwood products. Any primary product, such as lumber, poles, pilings, pulp, or fuelwood that is produced from roundwood.

Salvable dead trees. Standing or downed dead trees that were formerly growing stock and considered merchantable. Trees must be at least 5.0 inches d.b.h. to qualify.

Saplings. Live trees 1.0 to 5.0 inches d.b.h.

Saw log. A roundwood product, usually 8 feet in length or longer, processed into a variety of sawn products such as lumber, cants, pallets, railroad ties, and timbers.

Saw-log portion. The part of the bole of sawtimber trees between a 1-foot stump and the saw-log top.

Saw-log top. The point on the bole of sawtimber trees above which a conventional saw log cannot be produced. The minimum saw-log top is 7.0 inches d.o.b. for softwoods and 9.0 inches d.o.b. for hardwoods.

Sawtimber-size trees. Softwoods 9.0 inches d.b.h. and larger and hardwoods 11.0 inches d.b.h. and larger.

Sawtimber volume. Growing-stock volume in the saw-log portion of sawtimber-sized trees in board feet (International ¼-inch rule).

Seedlings. Trees <1.0 inch d.b.h. and >1 foot tall for hardwoods, >6 inches tall for softwood, and >0.5 inch in diameter at ground level for longleaf pine.

Softwoods. Coniferous trees, usually evergreen, having leaves that are needles or scalelike.

Standard cord. A unit of measure applied to roundwood, usually bolts or split wood. It is a stack of wood 4 feet high, 4 feet wide, and 8 feet long encompassing 128 cubic feet of wood, bark, and air space. This usually translates to approximately 75.0 to 81.0 cubic feet of solid wood for pulpwood, because pulpwood is more uniform.

Standard unit. A unit measure applied to roundwood timber products. Board feet (International ¼-inch rule) is the standard unit used for saw logs and veneer; cords are used for pulpwood, composite panel, and fuelwood; hundred pieces for poles; thousand pieces for posts; and thousand cubic feet for all other miscellaneous forest products.

Timberland. Forest land capable of producing 20 cubic feet of industrial wood per acre per year and not withdrawn from timber utilization.

Timber product output. The total volume of roundwood products from all sources plus the volume of byproducts recovered from mill residues (equals roundwood product drain).

Timber products. Roundwood products and byproducts.

Timber removals. The total volume of trees removed from the timberland inventory by harvesting, cultural operations such as stand improvement, land clearing, or changes in land use. (Note: Includes roundwood products, logging residues, and other removals.)

Tree. Woody plant having one erect perennial stem or trunk at least 3 inches d.b.h., a more or less definitely formed crown of foliage, and a height of at least 13 feet (at maturity).

Upper-stem portion. The part of the main stem of sawtimber trees above the saw-log top and the minimum top diameter of 4.0 inches outside bark, or to the point where the main stem breaks into limbs.

Utilization studies. Studies conducted on active logging operations to develop factors for merchantable portions of trees left in the woods (logging residues), logging damage, and utilization of the unmerchantable portion of growing-stock trees and nongrowing-stock trees.

Veneer log. A roundwood product either rotary cut, sliced, stamped, or sawn into a variety of veneer products such as plywood, finished panels, veneer sheets, or sheathing.

Weight. A unit of measure for mill residues, expressed as oven-dry tons (2,000 oven-dry pounds).

Appendix

Index of Tables

Table A.1—Harvest and utilization volume by species group, source, and volume type, Georgia, 2009

Species group and source	Total tree volume	Growing stock					Nongrowing stock				
		Total	Saw log		Upper stem		Total	Stumps		Tops/limbs	
			Utilized	Not utilized	Utilized	Not utilized		Utilized	Not utilized	Utilized	Not utilized
						cubic feet					
Softwood											
Sawtimber	21,100.61	18,655.39	16,929.25	283.87	979.04	463.23	2,445.22	380.67	451.12	87.41	1,526.02
Poletimber	4,927.68	3,986.46	—	—	3,961.28	25.18	941.22	171.47	112.42	440.78	216.55
Total	26,028.29	22,641.85	16,929.25	283.87	4,940.32	488.41	3,386.44	552.14	563.54	528.19	1,742.57
Hardwood											
Sawtimber	11,847.55	9,769.40	8,166.97	297.92	756.88	547.63	2,078.15	119.05	421.05	29.83	1,508.22
Poletimber	2,410.21	1,904.82	—	—	1,832.97	71.85	505.39	68.48	93.51	110.06	233.34
Total	14,257.76	11,674.22	8,166.97	297.92	2,589.85	619.48	2,583.54	187.53	514.56	139.89	1,741.56

— = no sample for the cell.

Table A.2—Volume of softwood growing stock by product and utilization for sawtimber and poletimber, Georgia, 2009

Product	Total volume utilized	Growing stock			Nongrowing stock utilized	Saw-log portion			
		Total	Utilized	Not utilized		Total	Utilized	Cull utilized	Not utilized
					cubic feet				
Saw logs	11,672.89	11,770.89	11,329.49	441.40	343.40	10,371.45	10,194.96	172.11	4.38
Veneer logs	4,993.46	5,091.31	4,904.93	186.38	88.53	4,829.79	4,773.10	56.69	—
Composite panels	1,788.35	1,700.16	1,646.19	53.97	142.16	667.54	640.79	26.75	—
Pulpwood	3,117.59	2,733.67	2,686.03	47.64	431.56	392.51	380.26	12.24	—
Poles	968.89	980.01	943.93	36.08	24.96	919.38	909.09	10.29	—
Fence posts	408.73	365.82	359.01	6.81	49.72	32.45	31.04	1.41	—
Fuelwood	—	—	—	—	—	—	—	—	—
Total	22,949.91	22,641.86	21,869.58	772.28	1,080.33	17,213.12	16,929.24	279.49	4.38

Numbers in rows and columns may not sum to totals due to rounding.
— = no sample for the cell.

Table A.3—Percent of overutilization and underutilization for softwood growing stock by product for sawtimber and poletimber, Georgia, 2009

	Overutilization		Underutilization		Saw-log portion		
Product	Growing stock utilized/total volume utilized	Nongrowing stock utilized/total volume utilized	Growing stock utilized/total growing-stock volume	Growing stock not utilized/total growing-stock volume	Saw log utilized/total saw-log volume	Cull utilized/total saw-log volume	Saw log not utilized/total saw-log volume
				percent			
Saw logs	97.06	2.94	96.25	3.75	98.30	1.66	0.04
Veneer logs	98.23	1.77	96.34	3.66	98.83	1.17	—
Composite panels	92.05	7.95	96.83	3.17	95.99	4.01	—
Pulpwood	86.16	13.84	98.26	1.74	96.88	3.12	—
Poles	97.42	2.58	96.32	3.68	98.88	1.12	—
Fence posts	87.84	12.16	98.14	1.86	95.65	4.35	—
Fuelwood	—	—	—	—	—	—	—
All products	95.29	4.71	96.59	3.41	98.35	1.62	0.03

— = no sample for the cell.

Table A.4—Volume of softwood growing stock by product and utilization for sawtimber, Georgia, 2009

		Growing stock				Saw-log portion			
Product	Total volume utilized	Total	Utilized	Not utilized	Nongrowing stock utilized	Total	Utilized	Cull utilized	Not utilized
					cubic feet				
Saw logs	11,081.90	11,220.55	10,783.37	437.18	298.53	10,371.45	10,194.96	172.11	4.38
Veneer logs	4,993.46	5,091.31	4,904.93	186.38	88.53	4,829.79	4,773.10	56.69	—
Composite panels	788.61	809.50	763.26	46.24	25.35	667.54	640.79	26.75	—
Pulpwood	497.23	507.44	469.47	37.97	27.76	392.51	380.26	12.24	—
Poles	968.89	980.01	943.93	36.08	24.96	919.38	909.09	10.29	—
Fence posts	46.29	46.59	43.34	3.25	2.95	32.45	31.04	1.41	—
Fuelwood	—	—	—	—	—	—	—	—	—
Total	18,376.38	18,655.40	17,908.30	747.10	468.08	17,213.12	16,929.24	279.49	4.38

Numbers in rows and columns may not sum to totals due to rounding.

— = no sample for the cell.

Table A.5—Percent of overutilization and underutilization for softwood growing stock by product for sawtimber, Georgia, 2009

Product	Overutilization		Underutilization		Saw-log portion		
	Growing stock utilized/ total volume utilized	Nongrowing stock utilized/ total volume utilized	Growing stock utilized/total growing-stock volume	Growing stock not utilized/ total growing- stock volume	Saw log utilized/total saw-log volume	Cull utilized/ total saw-log volume	Saw log not utilized/ total saw-log volume
	percent						
Saw logs	97.31	2.69	96.10	3.90	98.30	1.66	0.04
Veneer logs	98.23	1.77	96.34	3.66	98.83	1.17	—
Composite panels	96.79	3.21	94.29	5.71	95.99	4.01	—
Pulpwood	94.42	5.58	92.52	7.48	96.88	3.12	—
Poles	97.42	2.58	96.32	3.68	98.88	1.12	—
Fence posts	93.63	6.37	93.02	6.98	95.65	4.35	—
Fuelwood	—	—	—	—	—	—	—
All products	97.45	2.55	96.00	4.00	98.35	1.62	0.03

— = no sample for the cell.

Table A.6—Volume of softwood growing stock by product and utilization for poletimber, Georgia, 2009

Product	Total volume utilized	Growing stock			Nongrowing stock utilized
		Total	Utilized	Not utilized	
		cubic feet			
Saw logs	590.99	550.34	546.12	4.22	44.87
Veneer logs	—	—	—	—	—
Composite panels	999.74	890.66	882.93	7.73	116.81
Pulpwood	2,620.36	2,226.23	2,216.56	9.67	403.80
Poles	—	—	—	—	—
Fence posts	362.44	319.23	315.67	3.56	46.77
Fuelwood	—	—	—	—	—
Total	4,573.53	3,986.46	3,961.28	25.18	612.25

Numbers in rows and columns may not sum to totals due to rounding.

— = no sample for the cell.

Table A.7—Percent of overutilization and underutilization for softwood growing stock by product for poletimber, Georgia, 2009

	Overutilization		Underutilization	
Product	Growing stock utilized/ total volume utilized	Nongrowing stock utilized/ total volume utilized	Growing stock utilized/total growing-stock volume	Growing stock not utilized/ total growing-stock volume
	percent			
Saw logs	92.41	7.59	99.23	0.77
Veneer logs	—	—	—	—
Composite panels	88.32	11.68	99.13	0.87
Pulpwood	84.59	15.41	99.57	0.43
Poles	—	—	—	—
Fence posts	87.10	12.90	98.88	1.12
Fuelwood	—	—	—	—
All products	86.61	13.39	99.37	0.63

— = no sample for the cell.

Table A.8—Volume of softwood cull by product and utilization, Georgia, 2009

		Nongrowing stock			
		Merchantable			
Product	Total volume utilized	Total	Utilized	Not utilized	Unmerchantable utilized
	cubic feet				
Saw logs	—	—	—	—	—
Veneer logs	—	—	—	—	—
Composite panels	59.49	56.81	56.57	0.24	2.92
Pulpwood	22.53	18.60	18.60	—	3.93
Poles	—	—	—	—	—
Fence posts	—	—	—	—	—
Fuelwood	—	—	—	—	—
Total	82.02	75.41	75.17	0.24	6.85

Numbers in rows and columns may not sum to totals due to rounding.
— = no sample for the cell.

Table A.9—Percent of overutilization and underutilization for softwood cull by product, Georgia, 2009

| | Overutilization | | Underutilization | |
| | Merchantable utilized/ total volume utilized | Unmerchantable utilized/ total volume utilized | Merchantable utilized/total merchantable volume | Merchantable not utilized/ total merchantable volume |
Product				
	percent			
Saw logs	—	—	—	—
Veneer logs	—	—	—	—
Composite panels	95.09	4.91	99.58	0.42
Pulpwood	82.56	17.44	100.00	—
Poles	—	—	—	—
Fence posts	—	—	—	—
Fuelwood	—	—	—	—
All products	91.65	8.35	99.68	0.32

— = no sample for the cell.

Table A.10—Volume of hardwood growing stock by product and utilization for sawtimber and poletimber, Georgia, 2009

| | Total volume utilized | Growing stock | | | Nongrowing stock utilized | Saw-log portion | | | |
| | | Total | Utilized | Not utilized | | Total | Utilized | Cull utilized | Not utilized |
Product									
	cubic feet								
Saw logs	8,661.68	9,303.66	8,528.58	775.08	133.10	7,983.45	7,717.64	104.85	160.96
Veneer logs	—	—	—	—	—	—	—	—	—
Composite panels	68.65	70.41	62.92	7.49	5.73	31.13	28.48	2.65	—
Pulpwood	2,206.18	2,165.45	2,034.81	130.64	171.37	450.30	420.84	28.04	1.43
Poles	—	—	—	—	—	—	—	—	—
Fence posts	—	—	—	—	—	—	—	—	—
Fuelwood	147.73	134.71	130.51	4.20	17.22	—	—	—	—
Total	11,084.24	11,674.23	10,756.82	917.41	327.42	8,464.88	8,166.96	135.54	162.39

Numbers in rows and columns may not sum to totals due to rounding.

— = no sample for the cell.

Table A.11—Percent of overutilization and underutilization for hardwood growing stock by product for sawtimber and poletimber, Georgia, 2009

Product	Overutilization		Underutilization		Saw-log portion		
	Growing stock utilized/ total volume utilized	Nongrowing stock utilized/ total volume utilized	Growing stock utilized/total growing-stock volume	Growing stock not utilized/ total growing-stock volume	Saw log utilized/ total saw-log volume	Cull utilized/ total saw-log volume	Saw log not utilized/ total saw-log volume
	percent						
Saw logs	98.46	1.54	91.67	8.33	96.67	1.31	2.02
Veneer logs	—	—	—	—	—	—	—
Composite panels	91.65	8.35	89.36	10.64	91.49	8.51	—
Pulpwood	92.23	7.77	93.97	6.03	93.46	6.23	0.32
Poles	—	—	—	—	—	—	—
Fence posts	—	—	—	—	—	—	—
Fuelwood	88.34	11.66	96.88	3.12	—	—	—
All products	97.05	2.95	92.14	7.86	96.48	1.60	1.92

— = no sample for the cell.

Table A.12—Volume of hardwood growing stock by product and utilization for sawtimber, Georgia, 2009

Product	Total volume utilized	Growing stock			Nongrowing stock utilized	Saw-log portion			
		Total	Utilized	Not utilized		Total	Utilized	Cull utilized	Not utilized
					cubic feet				
Saw logs	8,487.76	9,131.20	8,360.88	770.32	126.88	7,983.45	7,717.64	104.85	160.96
Veneer logs	—	—	—	—	—	—	—	—	—
Composite panels	39.11	44.25	38.49	5.76	0.62	31.13	28.48	2.65	—
Pulpwood	545.86	593.95	524.48	69.47	21.38	450.30	420.84	28.04	1.43
Poles	—	—	—	—	—	—	—	—	—
Fence posts	—	—	—	—	—	—	—	—	—
Fuelwood	—	—	—	—	—	—	—	—	—
Total	9,072.73	9,769.40	8,923.85	845.55	148.88	8,464.88	8,166.96	135.54	162.39

Numbers in rows and columns may not sum to totals due to rounding.

— = no sample for the cell.

Table A.13—Percent of overutilization and underutilization for hardwood growing stock by product for sawtimber, Georgia, 2009

Product	Overutilization		Underutilization		Saw-log portion		
	Growing stock utilized/ total volume utilized	Nongrowing stock utilized/ total volume utilized	Growing stock utilized/total growing-stock volume	Growing stock not utilized/ total growing-stock volume	Saw log utilized/ total saw-log volume	Cull utilized/ total saw-log volume	Saw log not utilized/ total saw-log volume
	percent						
Saw logs	98.51	1.49	91.56	8.44	96.67	1.31	2.02
Veneer logs	—	—	—	—	—	—	—
Composite panels	98.41	1.59	86.98	13.02	91.49	8.51	—
Pulpwood	96.08	3.92	88.30	11.70	93.46	6.23	0.32
Poles	—	—	—	—	—	—	—
Fence posts	—	—	—	—	—	—	—
Fuelwood	—	—	—	—	—	—	—
All products	98.36	1.64	91.34	8.66	96.48	1.60	1.92

— = no sample for the cell.

Table A.14—Volume of hardwood growing stock by product and utilization for poletimber, Georgia, 2009

Product	Total volume utilized	Growing stock			Nongrowing stock utilized
		Total	Utilized	Not utilized	
		cubic feet			
Saw logs	173.92	172.46	167.70	4.76	6.22
Veneer logs	—	—	—	—	—
Composite panels	29.54	26.16	24.43	1.73	5.11
Pulpwood	1,660.32	1,571.50	1,510.33	61.17	149.99
Poles	—	—	—	—	—
Fence posts	—	—	—	—	—
Fuelwood	147.73	134.71	130.51	4.20	17.22
Total	2,011.51	1,904.83	1,832.97	71.86	178.54

Numbers in rows and columns may not sum to totals due to rounding.

— = no sample for the cell.

Table A.15—Percent of overutilization and underutilization for hardwood growing stock by product for poletimber, Georgia, 2009

Product	Overutilization		Underutilization	
	Growing stock utilized/ total volume utilized	Nongrowing stock utilized/ total volume utilized	Growing stock utilized/total growing-stock volume	Growing stock not utilized/ total growing-stock volume
	percent			
Saw logs	96.42	3.58	97.24	2.76
Veneer logs	—	—	—	—
Composite panels	82.70	17.30	93.39	6.61
Pulpwood	90.97	9.03	96.11	3.89
Poles	—	—	—	—
Fence posts	—	—	—	—
Fuelwood	88.34	11.66	96.88	3.12
All products	91.12	8.88	96.23	3.77

— = no sample for the cell.

Table A.16—Volume of hardwood cull by product and utilization, Georgia, 2009

Product	Total volume utilized	Nongrowing stock			
		Merchantable			
		Total	Utilized	Not utilized	Unmerchantable utilized
		cubic feet			
Saw logs	13.04	12.25	12.25	—	0.79
Veneer logs	—	—	—	—	—
Composite panels	10.14	11.25	10.06	1.19	0.08
Pulpwood	213.16	203.98	199.76	4.22	13.40
Poles	—	—	—	—	—
Fence posts	—	—	—	—	—
Fuelwood	10.35	11.09	9.76	1.33	0.59
Total	246.69	238.57	231.83	6.74	14.86

Numbers in rows and columns may not sum to totals due to rounding.

— = no sample for the cell.

Table A.17—Percent of overutilization and underutilization for hardwood cull by product, Georgia, 2009

Product	Overutilization		Underutilization	
	Merchantable utilized/ total volume utilized	Unmerchantable utilized/ total volume utilized	Merchantable utilized/total merchantable volume	Merchantable not utilized/total merchantable volume
	percent			
Saw logs	93.94	6.06	100.00	—
Veneer logs	—	—	—	—
Composite panels	99.21	0.79	89.42	10.58
Pulpwood	93.71	6.29	97.93	2.07
Poles	—	—	—	—
Fence posts	—	—	—	—
Fuelwood	94.30	5.70	88.01	11.99
All products	93.98	6.02	97.17	2.83

— = no sample for the cell.